Start With Just 3 Chords

by Ronald Herder

Contents

Introduction

Nothing sounds so great on the keyboard as a beautiful tune accompanied by rich chords. What a perfect combination!

Yet, chords are easy to find on the keyboard . . . they're easy to spot on the music page . . . and all of the chords in this book are very, very simple to finger.

Let's jump right into this great-sounding world of keyboard sound. We'll take it a step at a time, with just the right amount of explanation so that you'll know exactly what to do.

Every step along the way will have one goal and one goal only: to learn to make beautiful keyboard music by mastering those rich-sounding basic chords that you'll meet again and again in all kinds of music . . . in popular sheet music . . . in Broadway show tunes . . . in ragtime and the blues . . . and even in the most cherished classical pieces you've always loved and wanted to play. Let's do it!

Easy Steps to Chords

A chord is the sound you make when you strike two or more keys <u>at the</u> <u>same time.</u>

You can play chords with the *right* hand alone . . .

. . . or with the *left* hand alone . . .

. . . or with *both* hands playing together—

Warmup with Chords in the Right Hand

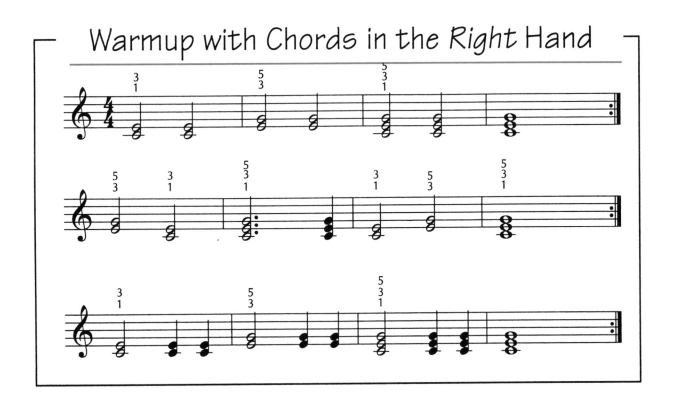

Warmup with Chords in the Left Hand

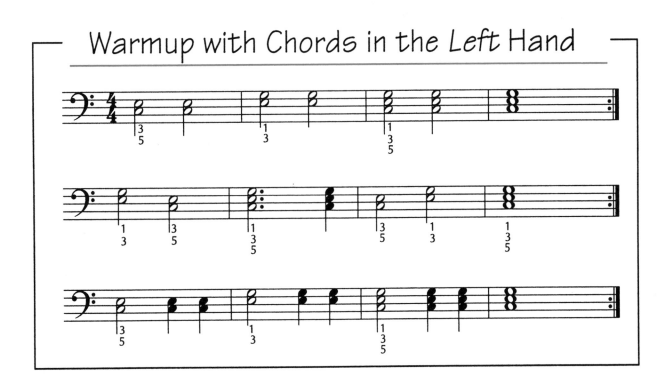

Harmonious Blends
Playing a Triad

The

C MAJOR TRIAD

is a harmonious blend

of

C – E – G

played together to make a three-note chord.

C MAJOR TRIAD
ON THE KEYBOARD

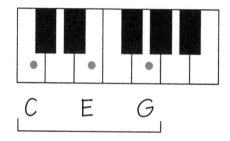

C   E   G

C MAJOR TRIAD
ON THE MUSIC STAFF

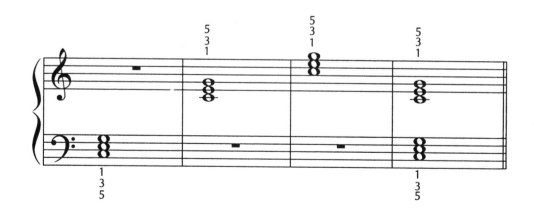

Fanfare

- Notes that are written one above the other are struck at <u>exactly</u> the same time.
- Listen to yourself strike each chord, first with the right hand, then with the left.
- Be your own audience. Be your own critic.

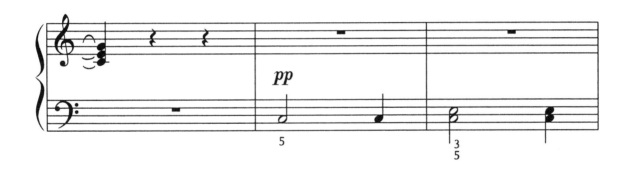

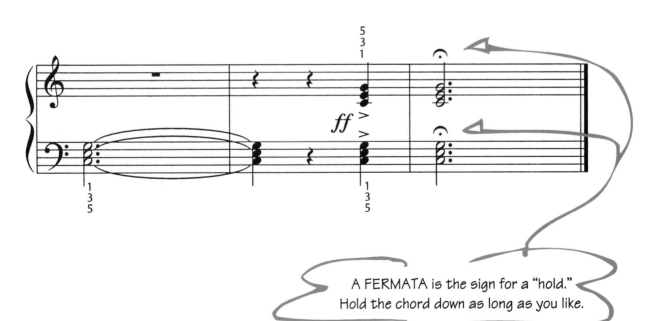

A FERMATA is the sign for a "hold."
Hold the chord down as long as you like.

Playing "Frère Jacques"

The familiar old French folk song called "Frère Jacques" uses that same C MAJOR TRIAD as a left-hand accompaniment.

It's easy to play and fun to hear, but first let's rehearse all the chords in this piece.

• Take your time.

• Strike the chord notes together to make a nice, rich sound.

• For those left-hand chords, remember to hold each whole note for 4 slow beats.

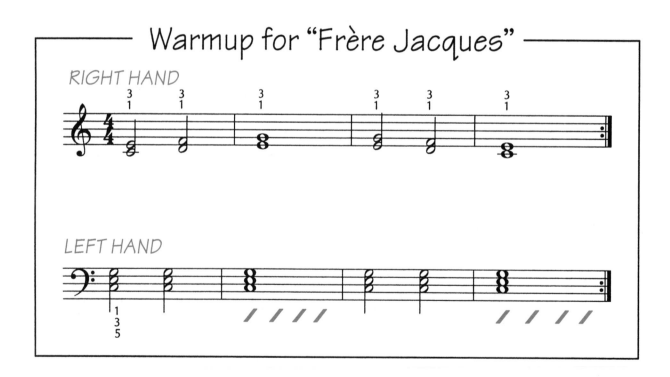

Frère Jacques

- As you play both hands together, listen to how the simple chord fits the melody so beautifully.
- Strike the notes of each three-note chord at exactly the same time. Exercise the same care for those rich two-note chords wherever they turn up. They'll sound great on any keyboard!

French Folk Song

Playing "Frère Jacques 2"

Now that you've played an old-fashioned "Frère Jacques," here comes one that's upside down!

This time the tune is in the left hand and the accompaniment—that same C MAJOR TRIAD—is in the right hand.

• As before, do the warmup first.

• Remember to strike chord notes at exactly the same time to make a solid, rich sound. This applies to those two-note chords as well as the triad.

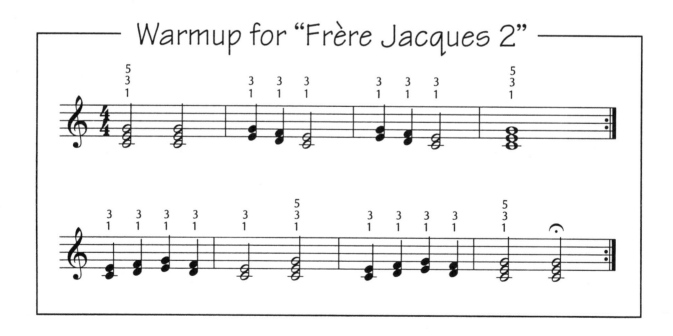

Frère Jacques 2

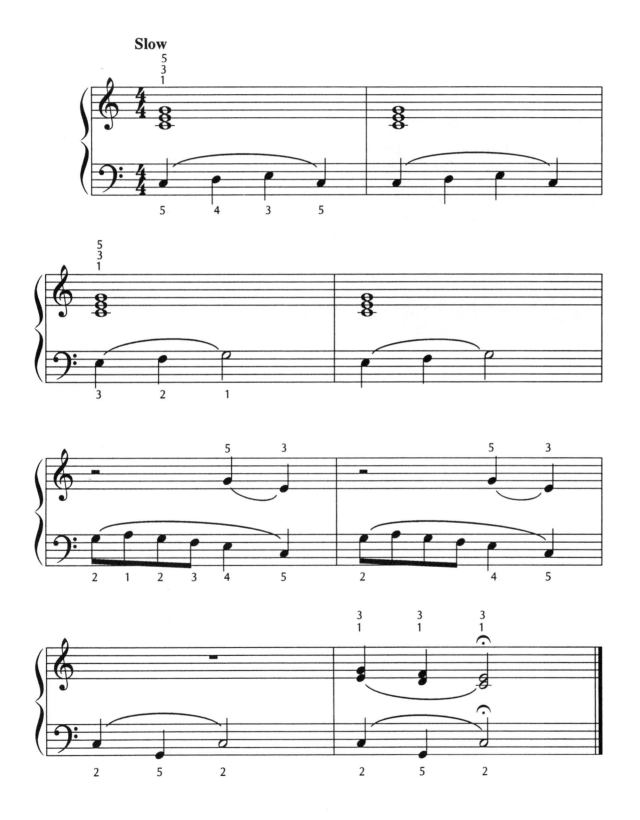

Some Chords Sit on Their Root . . .

Think of the C MAJOR TRIAD as a powerful tree with a strong root, a middle branch and an upper branch.

G is the upper branch.

E is the middle branch.

C, at the bottom, is the strong **root**.

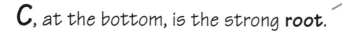

So this is a <u>ROOT-POSITION</u> TRIAD . . .

And *this* is a <u>ROOT-POSITION</u> TRIAD . . .

And *this* is a <u>ROOT-POSITION</u> TRIAD . . .

What do they have in common?

THE ROOT OF EACH TRIAD IS ON THE BOTTOM.

...But Some Chords Don't

Root-position triads have a great sound . . .

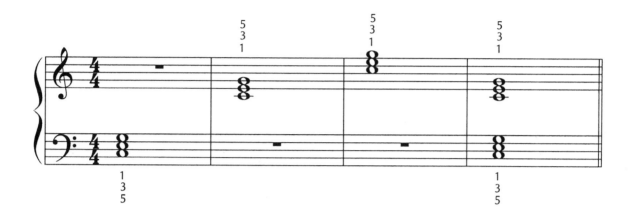

. . . but what a bore if we were stuck with them forever!

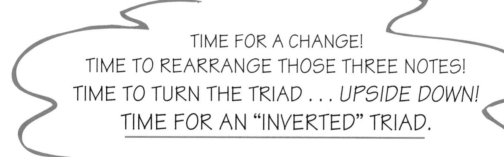

TIME FOR A CHANGE!
TIME TO REARRANGE THOSE THREE NOTES!
TIME TO TURN THE TRIAD . . . *UPSIDE DOWN!*
TIME FOR AN "INVERTED" TRIAD.

Notice how the **C** (on the <u>bottom</u> of the stack) . . .

. . . travels to the <u>top</u> of the stack . . .

. . . leaving **E** on the <u>bottom</u>.

Playing the C MAJOR TRIAD and Its Inversion

With your *left* hand in the *bass*,
play this root-position C MAJOR TRIAD
followed by its INVERSION.

With your *right* hand in the *middle* of the keyboard,
play the same two chords again.

With *both* hands together,
play the same two chords
from *low to high* on the keyboard.

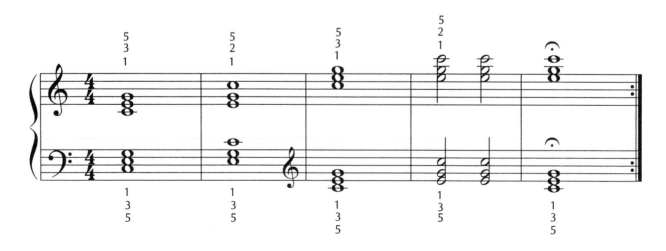

Prelude in C

The chord symbol C means:
"Play a *root-position* C MAJOR TRIAD.
C is on the bottom."

The chord symbol C/E means:
"Play an *inverted* C MAJOR TRIAD.
E is on the bottom."

Do what arrangers do! Write in the missing chord symbols.

Jack's Variation

Andante

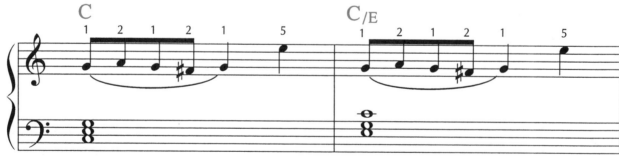

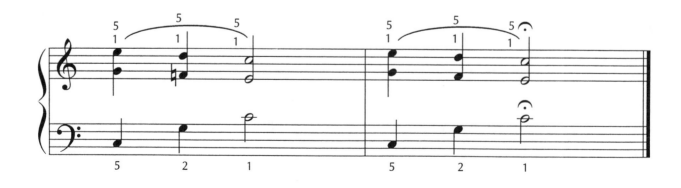

Ach, du lieber Augustin

Robust, not too fast

German Folk Dance-Song

Heigh-ho, the Derry-o!

"Love" is Never Having To Say . . .

Harmonious Blends 2
Playing the F MAJOR Triad

- C MAJOR is not the only triad on your keyboard.
  - Many other root-position triads exist all over the keyboard.
    - One of the new ones is the F MAJOR TRIAD.
      Let's add its new sound to your growing stock of chords.

The
F MAJOR TRIAD
is a harmonious blend
of
F – A – C
played together to make a three-note chord.

F MAJOR TRIAD
ON THE KEYBOARD

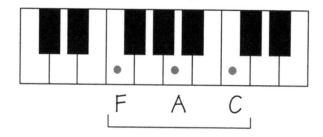

F   A   C

F MAJOR TRIAD
ON THE MUSIC STAFF

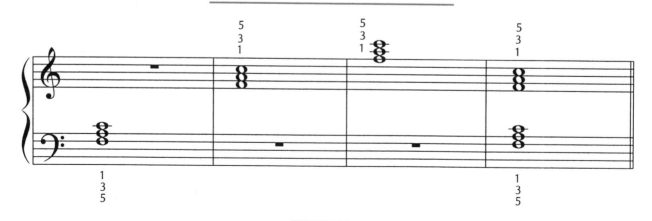

Fanfare 2

- Listen to yourself strike each chord, first with the right hand, then with the left.
- Be your own audience. Be your own critic.

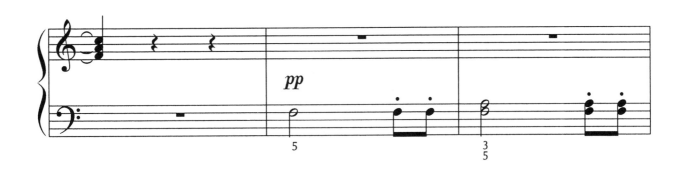

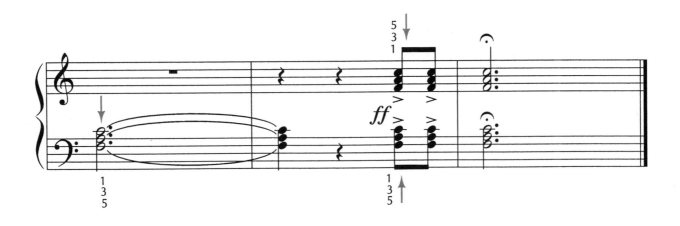

Taps

Traditional Bugle Call

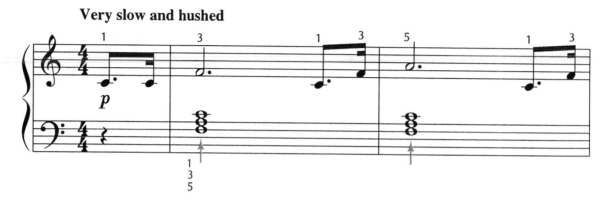

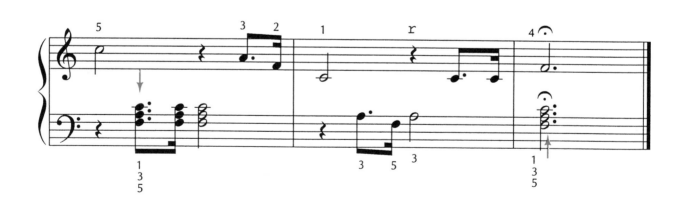

Au clair de la lune

"Spring"
from *The Four Seasons*

Antonio Vivaldi

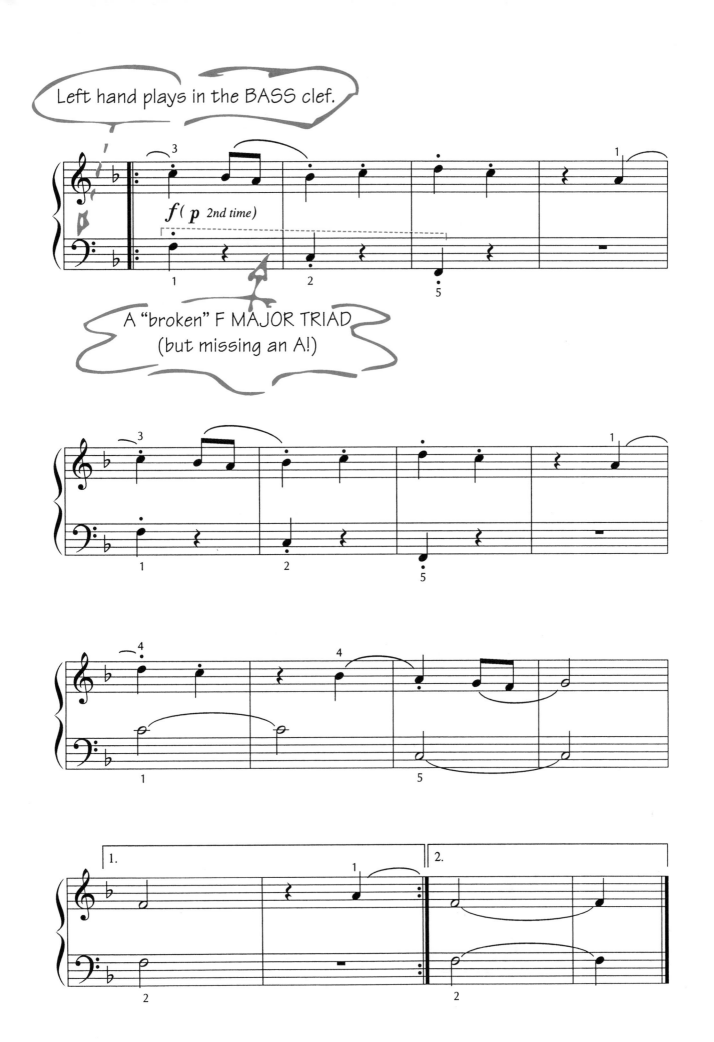

Making Music
with **C MAJOR** and **F MAJOR** Triads
Together

Cathedral at Sunset

- Take plenty of time to enjoy the rich sound and resonance
of these two triads in the same piece of music:
the C MAJOR TRIAD and the F MAJOR TRIAD
together in your hands!

Loch Lomond

Scottish Folk Song

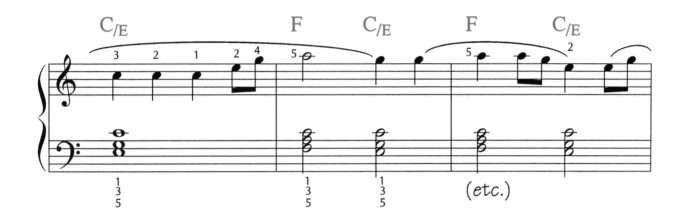

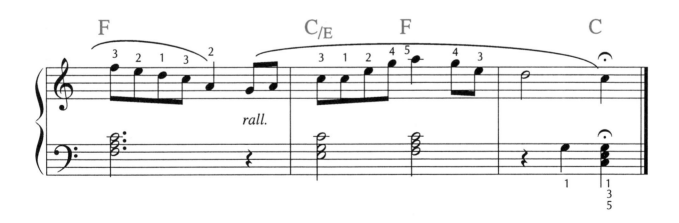

Amazing Grace

Very slow and quiet

Traditional

Depress the three keys firmly but softly,
Let your friends
and neighbors hear
that beautiful melody!

VISUALIZED CHORD DICTIONARY
(Each chord is shown in 2nd inversion)

35

major

minor

dim.

aug.

7th

6th

9th

m 7

Eency-Weency Spider

Bouncy

Nursery Song

Another kind of triad "breakup"

Suddenly slow and sad

Fast and bright again

"Breaking up" a chord

by playing

one note after the other

adds a great new sound

to your left-hand accompaniments.

Here's a left-hand warmup

with these arpeggios (are-PEHG-ee-ohz),

the Italian word that means "like a harp."

Slowly flowing

Mr. Clementi's Sonatina

Borrowed from Muzio Clementi's Sonatina in C, Op. 36, No. 1

Easy-going and gentle

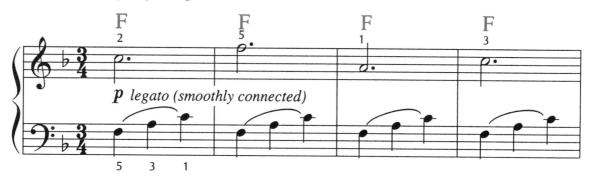

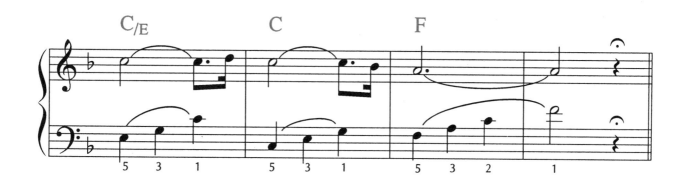

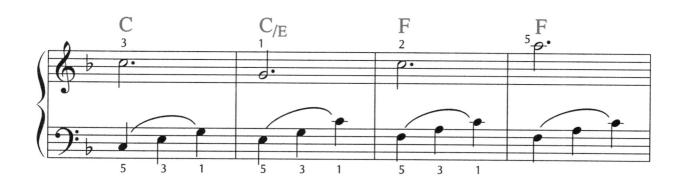

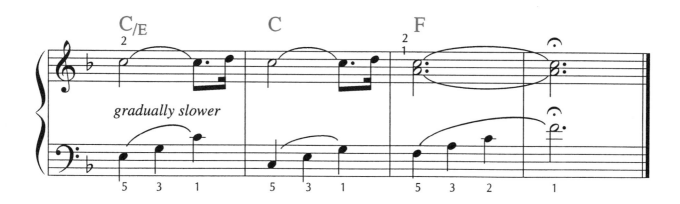

The Marines' Hymn

• Bang out those deep, thumpy left-hand chords like a set of drums—
Zum-zum zum! – precise and sharply *staccato* (short and dry).

Two reminders:
1. Play both hands in the **BASS** clef.
2. All **B**'s are flatted.

This **"8"** sign means:
"Play the left hand *one octave lower than written.*"

(etc.)

Playing the F MAJOR TRIAD and Its Inversion

With your *left* hand in the *bass*,
play this root-position F MAJOR TRIAD
followed by its INVERSION.

With your *right* hand in the *middle* of the keyboard,
play the same two chords again.

With *both* hands together,
play the same two chords
from *low to high* on the keyboard.

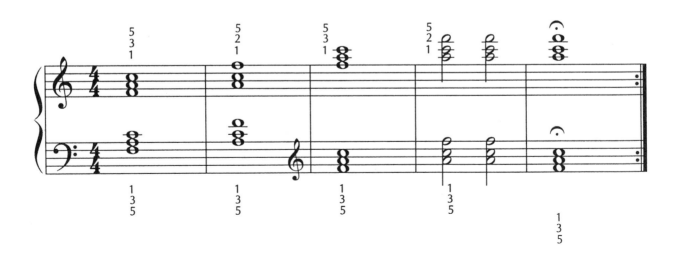

Prelude No. 2 in F

33

Home on the Range

Traditional Cowboy Song

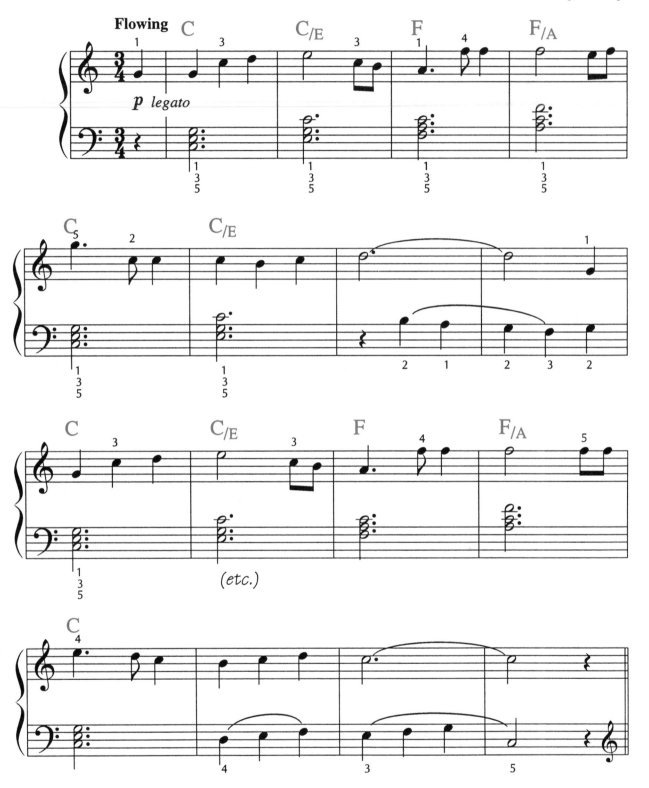

(etc.)

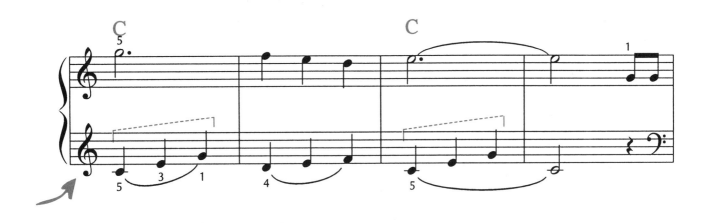

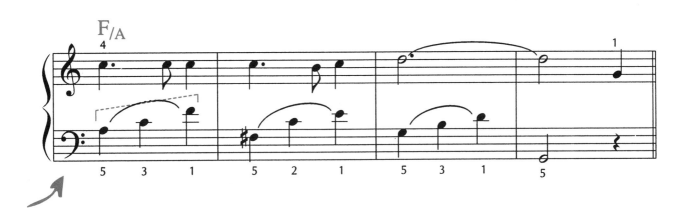

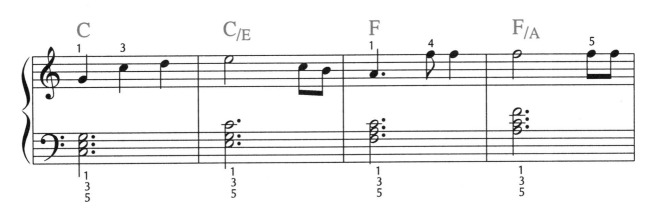

The Battle Cry of Freedom

American Marching Song

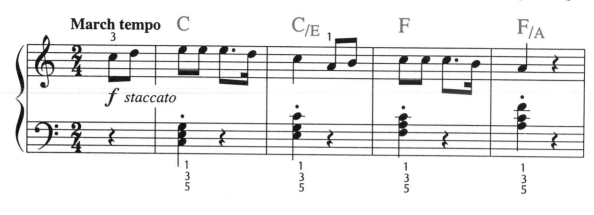

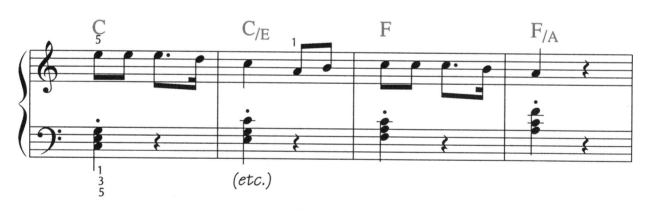

Light and airy, like a piccolo tune

p legato

Here's a s-t-r-e-t-c-h-e-d o-u-t C MAJOR arpeggio!

March again!

f

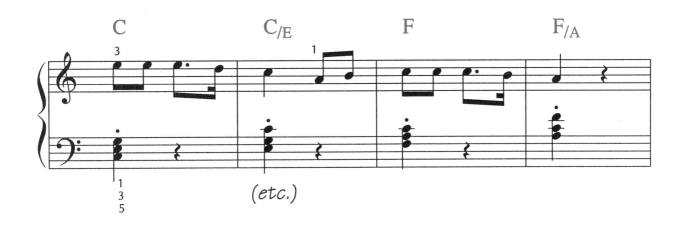

C   C/E   F   F/A

(etc.)

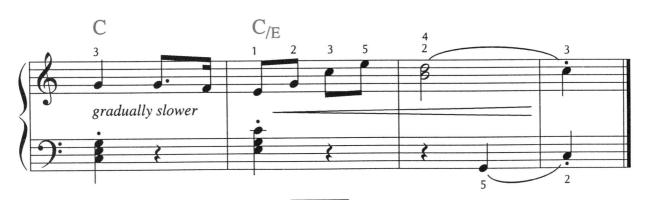

C   C/E

gradually slower

• ROUND 2 •

Here's another entertaining workout for your left hand.

But don't be staggered by that unfamiliar $\frac{3}{8}$ meter!

Just count a relaxed 1 - 2 - 3 for each bar.

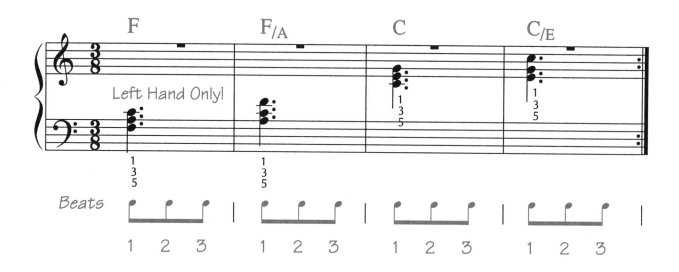

Easy-going, like a slow waltz

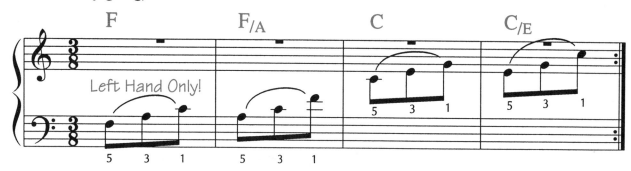

Sweet Molly Malone

("Cockles 'n' Mussels")

Irish Folk Song

Harmonious Blends 3
Playing the G MAJOR Triad

The
G MAJOR TRIAD
is a harmonious blend
of
G – B – D,
played together to make a three-note chord.

G MAJOR TRIAD
ON THE KEYBOARD

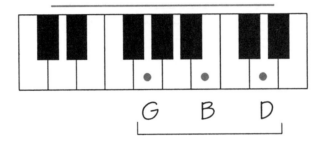

G   B   D

G MAJOR TRIAD
AND ITS INVERSION
ON THE MUSIC STAFF

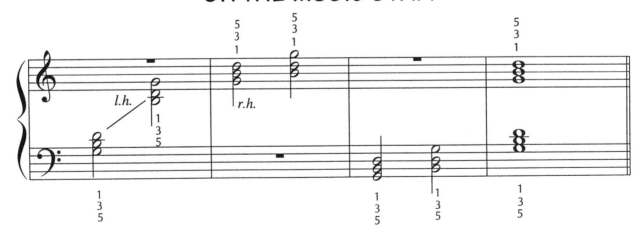

"Silence" Prelude in G

Rock of Ages

Traditional Hymn

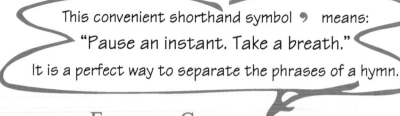

Home Sweet Home

• A delicate air with a quiet background of simple chords.
Keep an ear on your left hand so that it doesn't overshadow that sweet melody.

Words by John Howard Payne
Music adapted by Sir Henry Bishop

Shepherd's Song

Theme from Ludwig van Beethoven's Symphony No. 6
("Pastorale" Symphony)

- Once again, keep the chordal background as delicate and "out of the way" as possible.
  - A new touch of pedal for each chord change will help sustain the rich harmonies.

Là ci darem la mano

("Put your hand in mine")
Duet from Wolfgang Amadeus Mozart's opera *Don Giovanni*

- This is a great example of how triads can be broken up
  to make a rhythmic accompaniment:
First comes the *root* of each triad . . . then come the triad's *other* two notes.

"Hand-to-Hand Combat"
(Arpeggio Etude)

- An *étude* is a "study" that focuses on a particular technical feat.
This *étude* is about <u>passing arpeggios</u> from one hand to the other as smoothly as
possible. The tempo is up to you—so start slowly and evenly, until you get the hang of it.
Then feel free to rev up to any ridiculous speed your hands can manage!!!

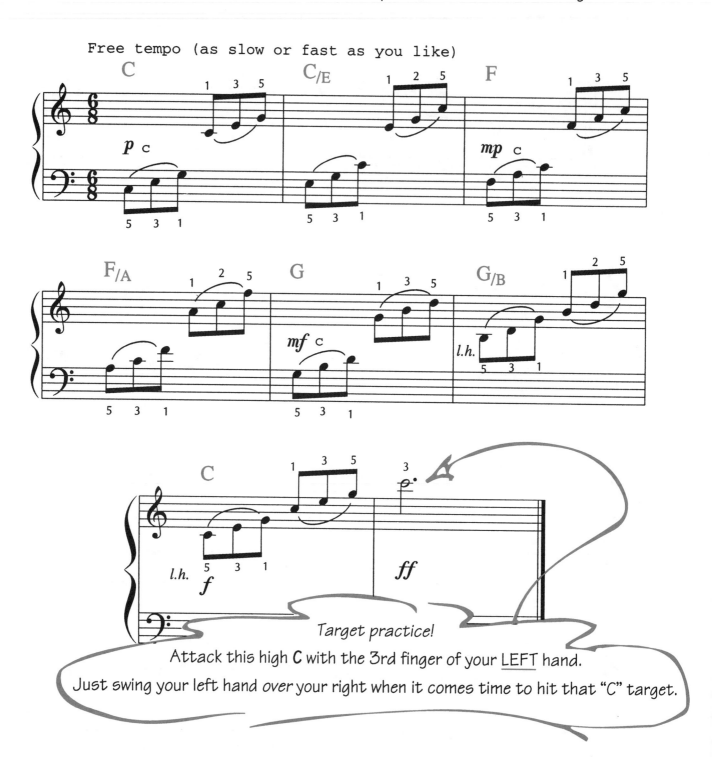

Target practice!
Attack this high **C** with the 3rd finger of your <u>LEFT</u> hand.
Just swing your left hand over your right when it comes time to hit that "C" target.

Etude in Blue

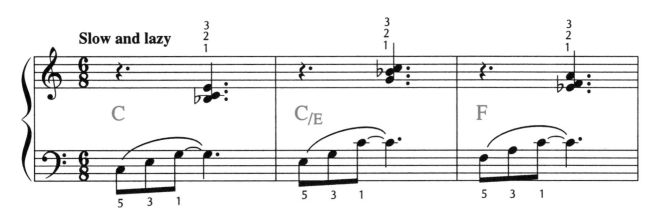

Slow and lazy

Pedal down for each bar.

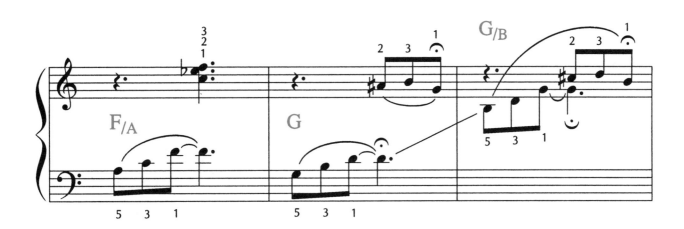

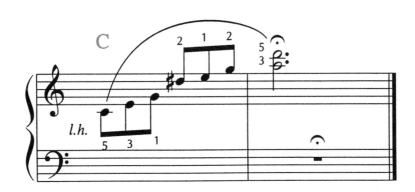

Topsy-Turvy
Upside-Down Triads

Root-position triads and inverted triads have a great sound . . .
. . . but . . . is . . . there . . . more . . . ?

TIME FOR ANOTHER CHANGE!
TIME TO REARRANGE THOSE THREE NOTES ONE MORE TIME!
TIME TO TURN THE TRIAD *EVEN MORE UPSIDE DOWN!*
TIME FOR A NEW KIND OF INVERTED TRIAD.

In the C MAJOR triad, notice how *both* the
C and E (on the bottom of the stack) . . .

. . . travel to the top of the stack . . .

. . . leaving *G* on the bottom.

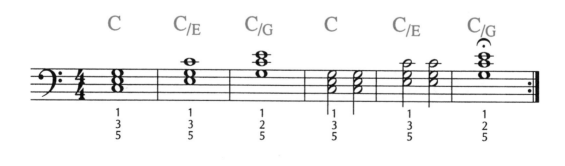

EASY PRACTICE SESSION WITH C/G

In the { F MAJOR } triad,

notice how *both* the

F and A (on the bottom of the stack) . . .

. . . travel to the top of the stack . . .

. . . leaving **C** on the bottom.

EASY PRACTICE SESSION WITH F/C

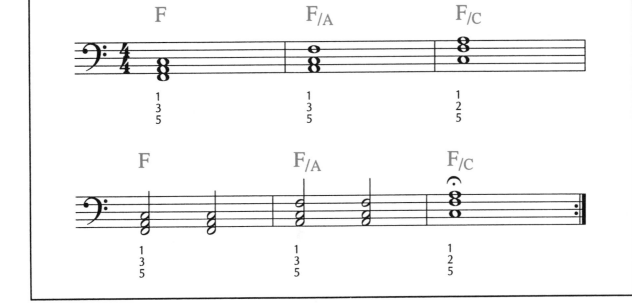

In the  triad,

notice how *both* the

G and B (on the <u>bottom</u> of the stack) . . .

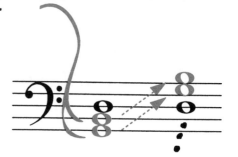

. . . travel to the <u>top</u> of the stack . . .

. . . leaving **D** on the bottom.

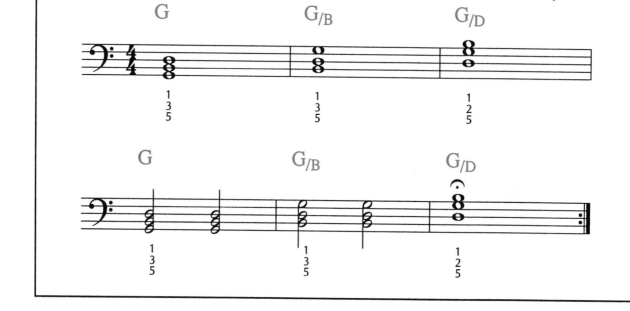

Sunrise

- Take plenty of time to play those softly rising left-hand chords.
- If you like, you can hold down the "loud" pedal while you play each set of chords.
  The pedal will help connect those rich keyboard sonorities.

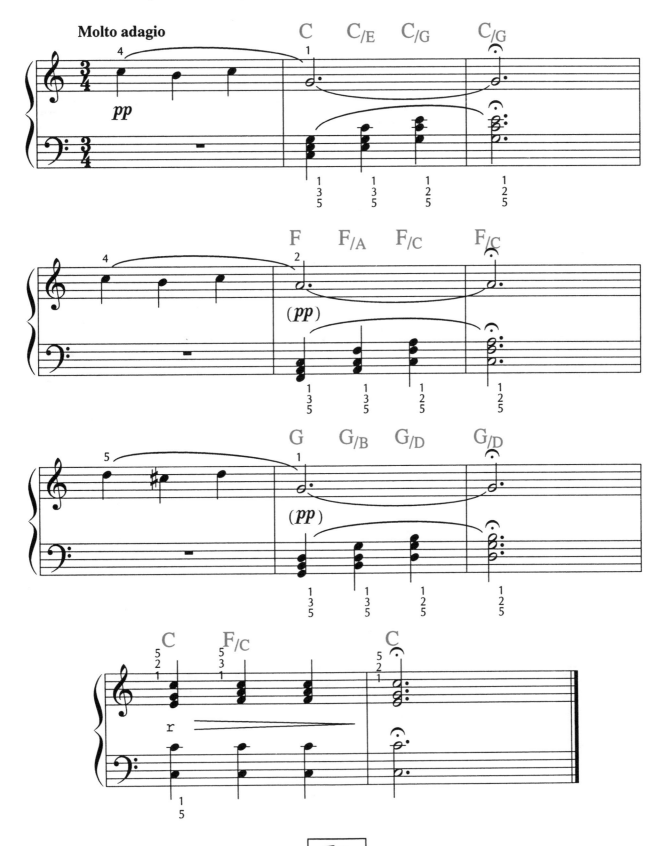

Bach's Minuet

Johann Sebastian Bach

Rock of Ages 2

Traditional Hymn

Square and sturdy

Drink to Me Only with Thine Eyes

English Traditional

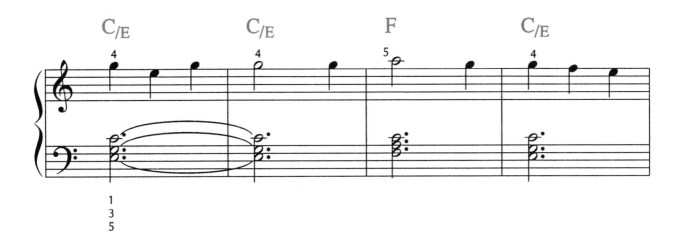

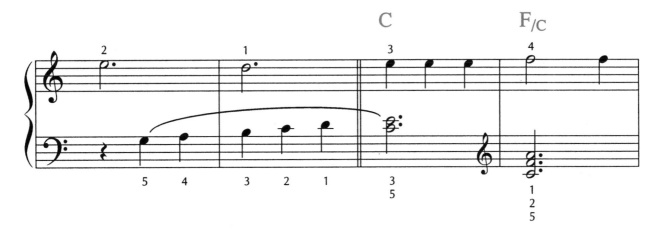

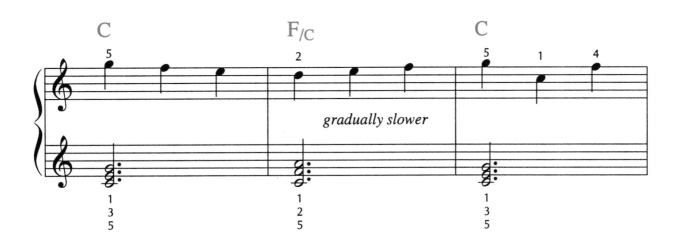

Ah! vous dirai-je, Maman?

Ah, what should I tell you, Mama?

("Twinkle, twinkle, little star")

Even Mozart loved this French folk song enough to compose
12 variations on its famous theme.

- For us, it's a great opportunity to play around with all three triads and their inversions.
  - As simple as this piece is, do what the pros do with a new work:
    <u>practice each hand separately . . . and s-l-o-w-l-y.</u>

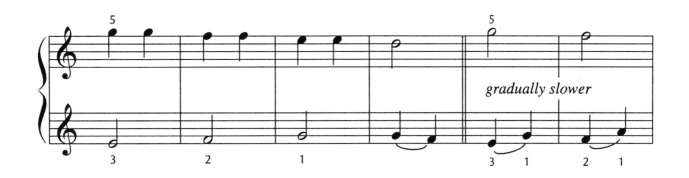

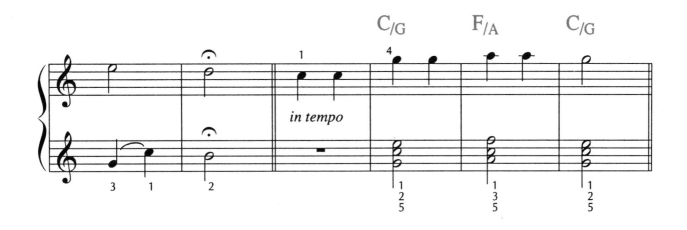

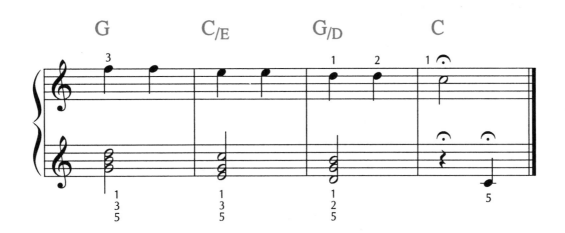

A Touch of the Blues

Making MINOR Triads

Where would we be without MINOR triads?

Nowhere!!!

No Blues. No sad love songs.

No touch of that extra-special color

in your growing rainbow of chords.

BUT...

Will you have to study *advanced rocket science*

to learn MINOR triads?

Will you have to know *brain surgery*

to learn MINOR triads?

Should you stop enjoying yourself and start worrying?

NO!

MINOR triads

are a snap to learn.

They are exactly (well, almost)

like the MAJOR triads

you already know —

but with one small change,

one tiny adjustment.

The  does it all.

Harmonious Blends 4
Playing the C MINOR TRIAD

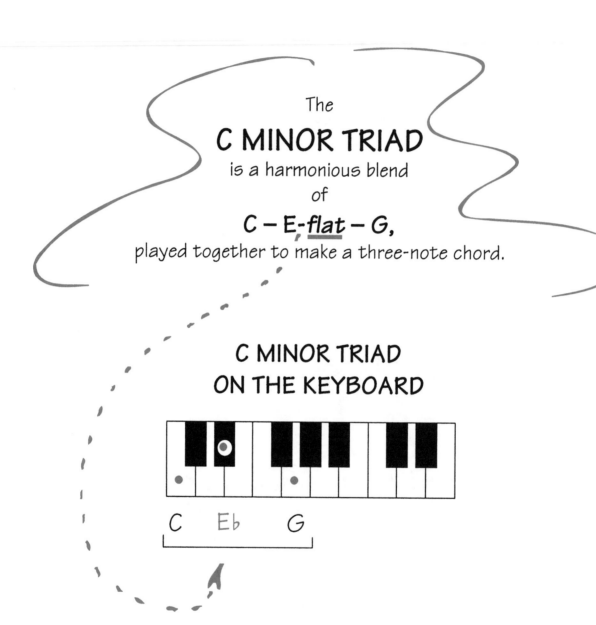

The
C MINOR TRIAD
is a harmonious blend
of
C – E-*flat* – G,
played together to make a three-note chord.

C MINOR TRIAD
ON THE KEYBOARD

C   Eb   G

Sweet Journey Blues

• This new Blues looks back to that great old standard "Sentimental Journey"
at the same time as it explores different left-hand combinations
of the new C MINOR TRIAD and the familiar F MAJOR TRIAD.

• And don't take those ♩. ♪ rhythms too literally.
Instead of a strict "classical" treatment, give that pattern a loose blues-y feel.

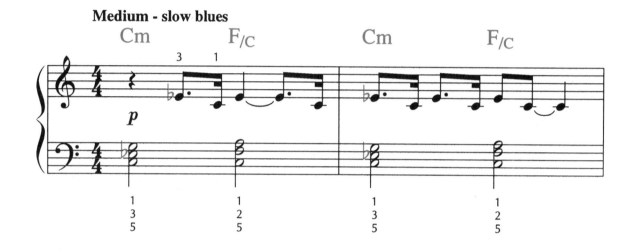

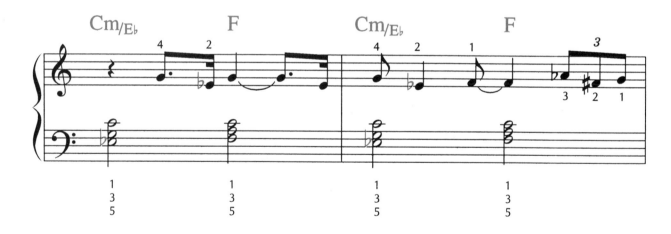

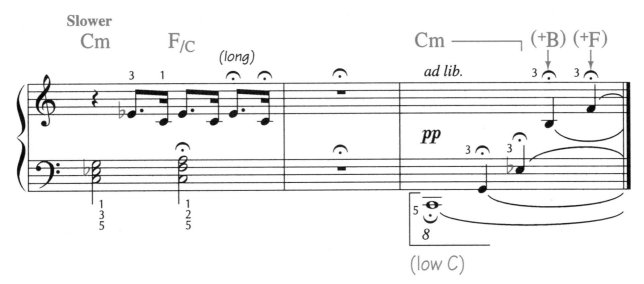

- Slow down a lot in the 3rd bar from the end.
- Then let that "silent" bar just sit there a moment.
- Finally, play that relaxed "free tempo" last bar, with the "loud" pedal down.

Take plenty of time to let those low rich keyboard sonorities hang in the air.

"Moonlight" Sonatina

- This miniature pays tribute to Beethoven's exquisite "Moonlight" Sonata,
  but on a very modest scale and in a much easier key.
  Let those endless triplets flow smoothly from note to note, and from beat to beat,
  like a gentle, unbroken stream of water.

- A simple way to keep count is to recite evenly:
  "ONE trip-let TWO trip-let ONE trip-let TWO trip-let" and so on.

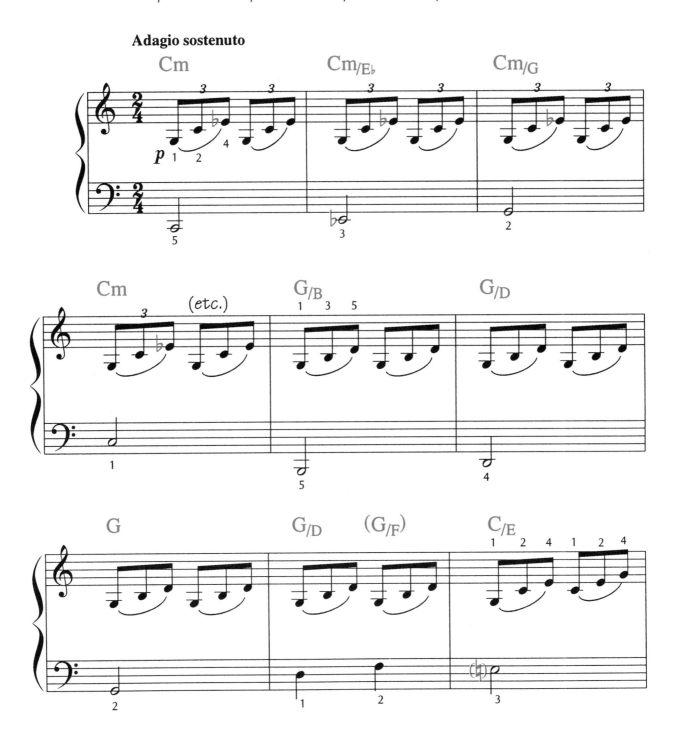

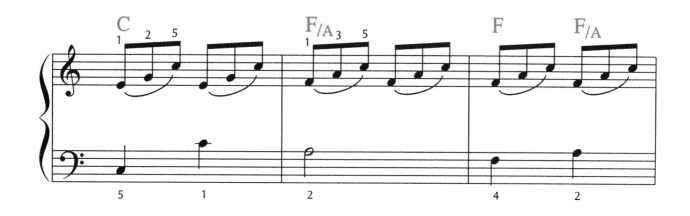

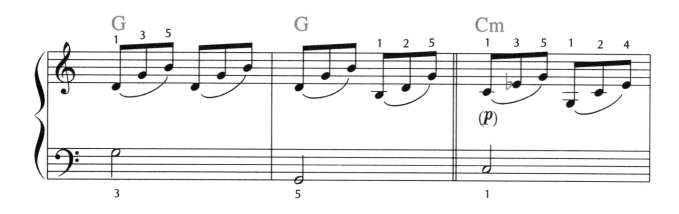

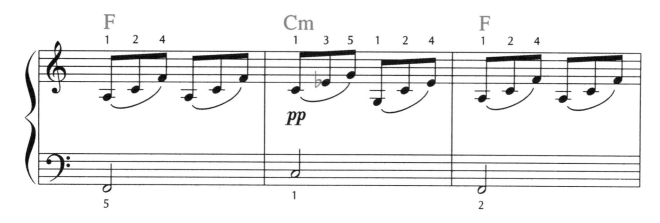

gradually slower until the end

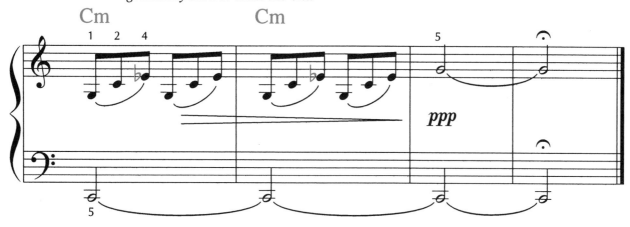

Harmonious Blends 5
Playing the F MINOR TRIAD

The
F MINOR TRIAD
is a harmonious blend
of
F – A-_flat_ – C,

played together to make a three-note chord.

**F MINOR TRIAD
ON THE KEYBOARD**

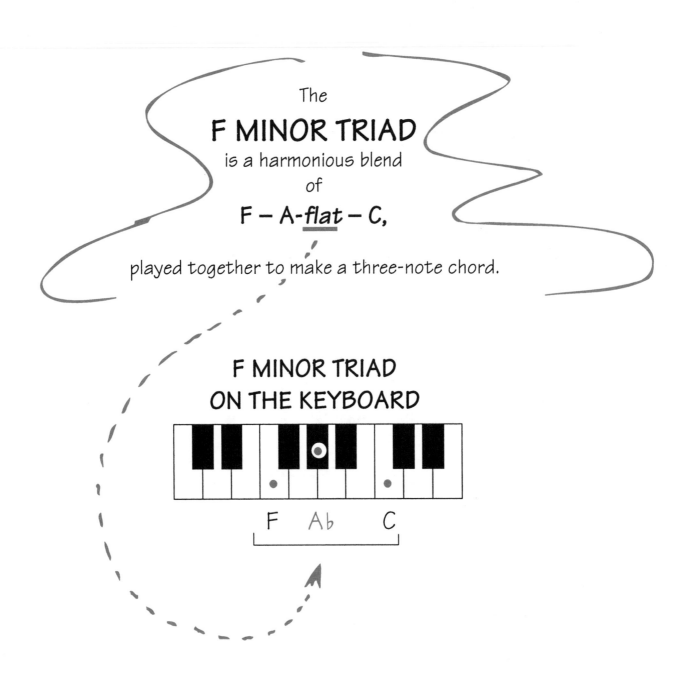

F   Ab   C

Slavic Lullaby

Quietly, plaintively

The Coventry Arpeggio Drill
But what went wrong?!?

Plenty! <u>There's not one single chord symbol on the page!</u>

Can you help out??? Can you save the day???

<u>Please fill in the missing chord symbol in each red box.</u>

Then run through this great left-hand finger-warmer for the piece that follows.

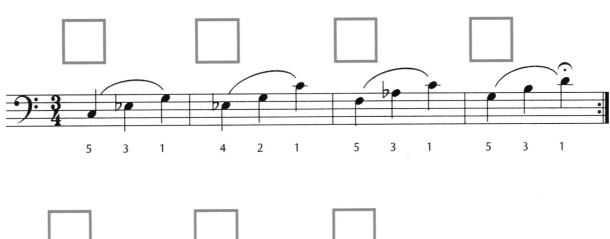

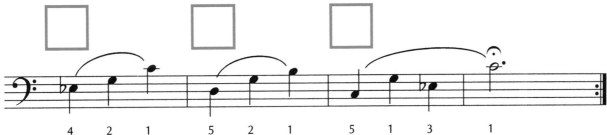

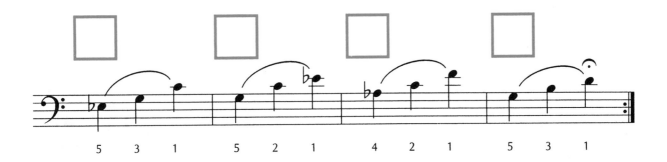

The Coventry Carol
(Lully, lullay)

Traditional English Christmas Song

Gently flowing

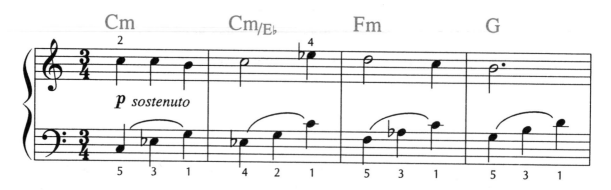

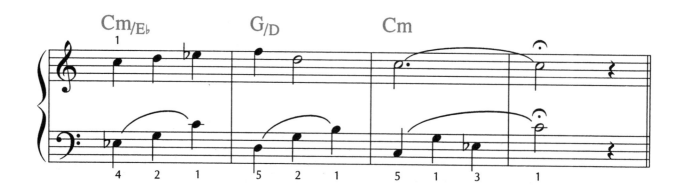

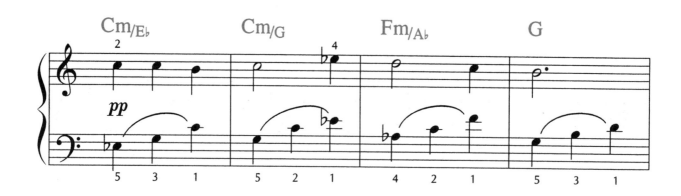

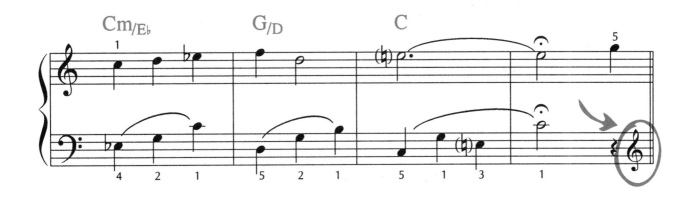

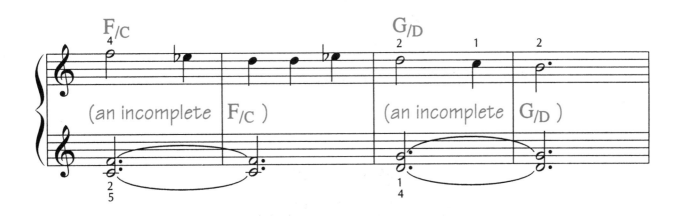

(an incomplete F/C)   (an incomplete G/D)

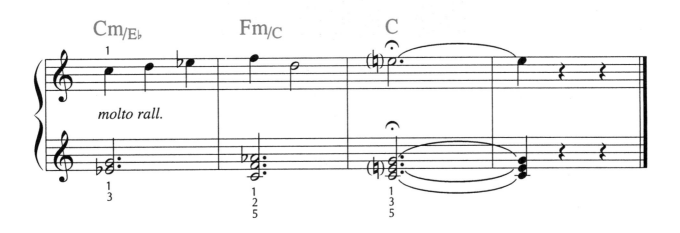

molto rall.

Harmonious Blends 6
Playing the G MINOR TRIAD

The
G MINOR TRIAD
is a harmonious blend
of
G – B-flat – D,

played together to make a three-note chord.

G MINOR TRIAD
ON THE KEYBOARD

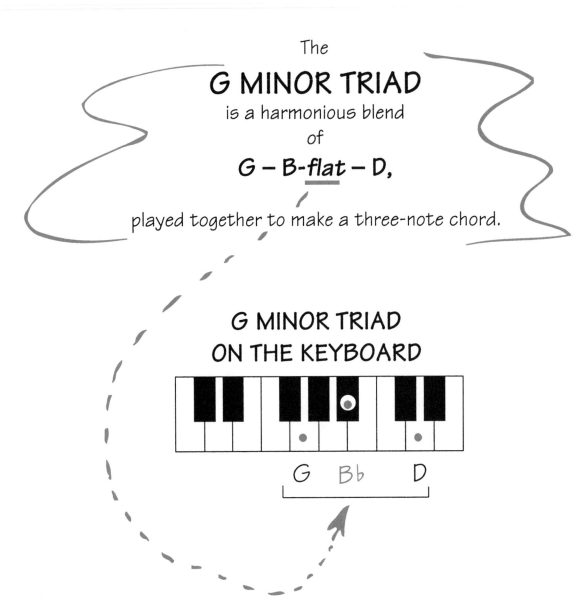

G   Bb   D

Black, black, black is the color of my true love's hair.
Those lips are like some rosy fair;
the purest eyes and the neatest hands,
I love the grass whereon she stands.

How I love my love and well she knows,
I love the grass whereon she goes;
when she on earth no more I see,
my life will quickly over be.

Quiet Meditation (I) on "Black is the Color"

Time to enjoy a few minutes of quiet and contemplation
with an unforgettable melody from America's Appalachian folk tradition.
Let the tempo be loose and free, without strictly kept note values.

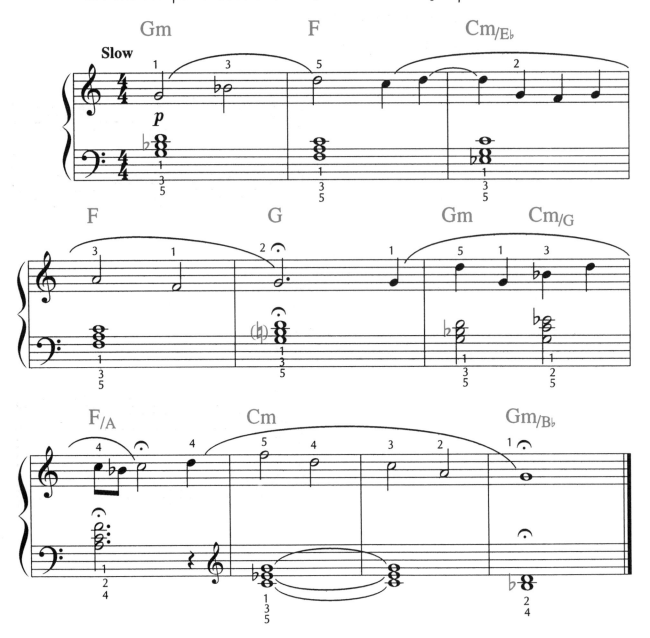

Quiet Meditation (II)
on "Black is the Color"

"Meditation II" presents the same music as "Meditation I,"
but this time with melody and harmonies written upside-down,
creating new sonorities and a slightly different, slightly jazzy, harmonic feeling.

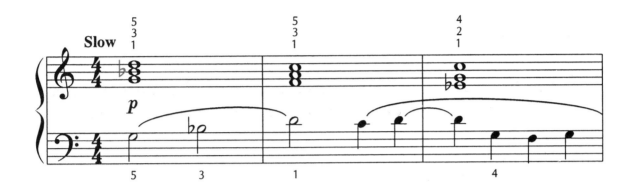

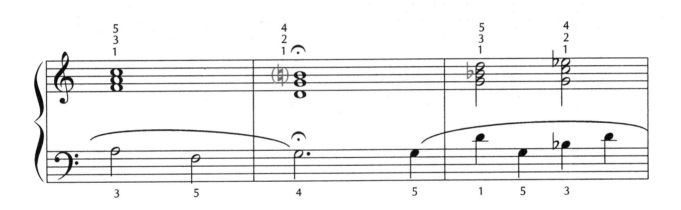

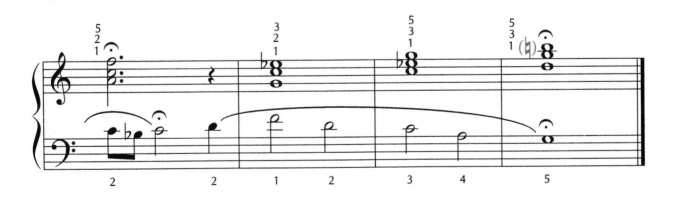

"Heigh-ho!"
March and Variation

- Step off bright and lively for this wonderful old march tune
  — but don't forget that even the pros practice
  s-l-o-w-l-y! s-l-o-w-l-y! s-l-o-w-l-y!
  when they encounter a new piece of music.

- Each "long pause" can be as long as you like before you jump right back into tempo.

- A brand-new (and easy) **D minor triad (D–F–A)** turns up twice in this piece;
  Take it right in stride as you master one new chord after the other!

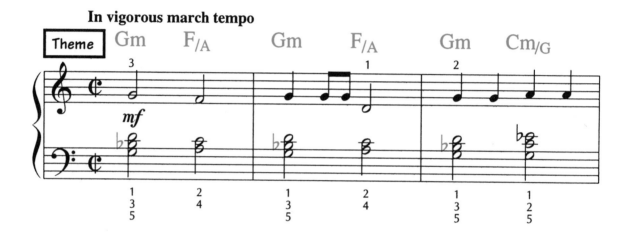

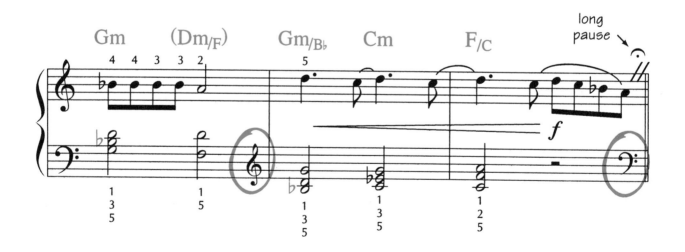

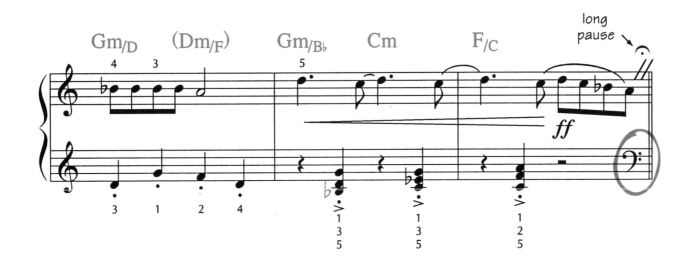

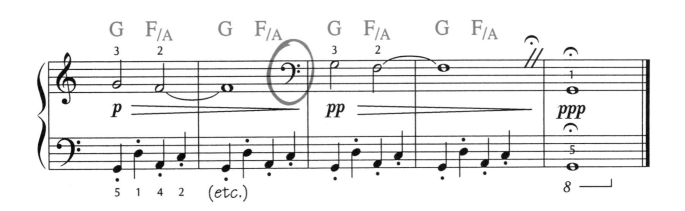

Grey Day, Strange Town

• As it's done for generations, the Blues wraps a plaintive, weary lament around the simplest chords in the world.

• Those left-hand chords are the familiar ones you know so well. You shouldn't have a bit of trouble with them.

• As for the right-hand melody, just listen to how those "bent" pitches and little inflections wind themselves playfully around the basic harmony. They're easy to play if you relax and let your feelings take over. That tune is full of old tears that dried up long ago.

Slow, lazy, worn-out Blues

Something Borrowed, Something Bluer

Musicians love the simple sound of the TRIAD.

But they also love to *color* it, *dress* it up,

make it *bluer, sweeter* or more *intense.*

They can do this

by

transforming

the

TRIAD

into a 7th CHORD.

7th CHORDS

are easy to learn and easy to play.

If you can picture growing

<u>ONE NEW BUD</u>

on top of an old tree,

you can picture adding

<u>ONE NEW NOTE</u>

on top of the familiar old triads

you know so well.

The

G⁷

is a sweet blend

of the G <u>MAJOR</u> triad

G – B – D

with a bluesy

F

"budding" 7 lines and spaces

above root **G**.

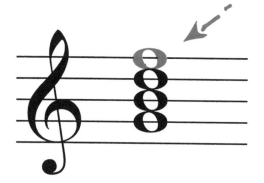

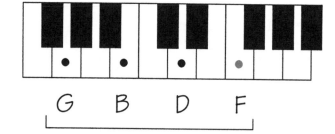

The

Gm⁷

is a sweet blend

of the G <u>MINOR</u> triad

G – B♭ – D

with a bluesy

F

"budding" 7 lines and spaces

above root **G**.

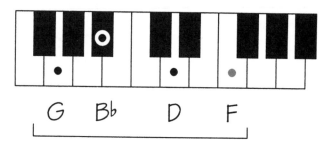

"Seven and Seven"

- Here are the first two bars of George and Ira Gershwin's great hit standard "The Man I Love."

- Listen to how the sweet G^7 and the bluesy Gm^7 gove the music a wonderful jazzy feeling.

- Relax and take your time as you play this in the key of G.

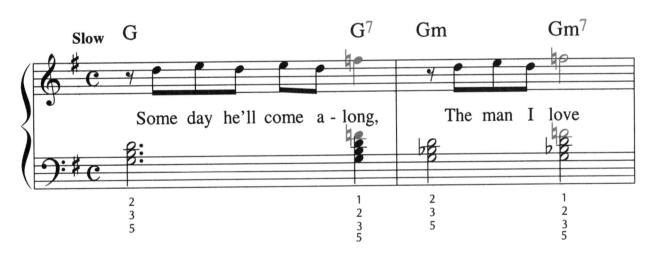

Now play exactly the same tune and harmonies,
this time transposed down to the key of F.

The key may have changed, but listen to how
those rich 7th chords still work their magic!

Remember that these new 7th chords
are nothing more than triads plus a new note
"budding" 7 lines and spaces above the root.

- Finally, play the same tune and harmonies,
now transposed down to the key of C.

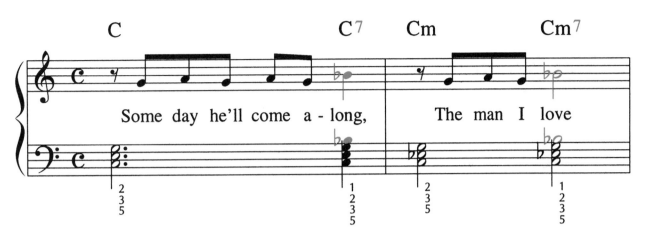

C   **C**⁷   **Cm**   **Cm**⁷

Some day he'll come a - long,   The man I love

Can you fill in the missing notes?
(The solution is printed below, upside down. Don't look!)

C⁷ **Cm**⁷   **C**⁷ **Cm**⁷

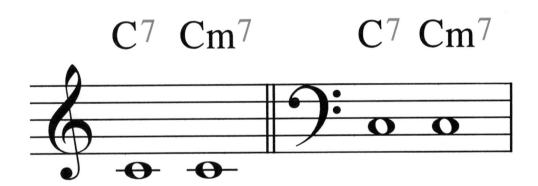

Ballin' the Jack

by Chris Smith and
James Reese Europe

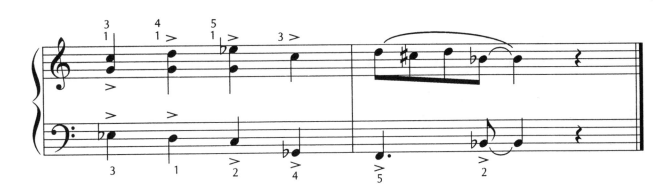

87

Kalinka I

This catchy and very appealing Russian folk song is harmonized with four chords:

- G7 and the C minor triad (in bars 1-8)
- then C7 and the F minor triad (in bars 9-16).

In this arrangement, all harmonies are in root position only.

Start slow, then get faster and faster, louder and louder.

Kalinka II

More variety this time, with the chords played in <u>different positions</u>.
Notice what's happened to the 7th chords. They now look like this:

G⁷

- 3rd inversion (**F** on the bottom)
- 2nd inversion (**D** on the bottom)
- 1st inversion (**B** on the bottom)
- Root position (**G** on the bottom)

C⁷

- 3rd inversion (**B-flat** on the bottom)
- 2nd inversion (**G** on the bottom)
- 1st inversion (**E** on the bottom)
- Root position (**C** on the bottom)

Start slow, then get faster and faster, louder and louder.

89

SIX PRETTY EASY, FAIRLY TYPICAL, GOOD-SOUNDING ACCOMPANIMENT PATTERNS FOUND IN CLASSICAL PIECES AND IN SHEET MUSIC OF ALL KINDS, DEMONSTRATING HOW THE 7TH CHORD IS USED IN ROOT POSITION AND ITS THREE INVERSIONS . . .

C7

Solid chords in the left hand make a full-sounding background for even the simplest tune. "Quiet Meditation III," page 92, is a perfect example. So are "Grey Day," page 96, and "The St. Louis Blues," page 98.

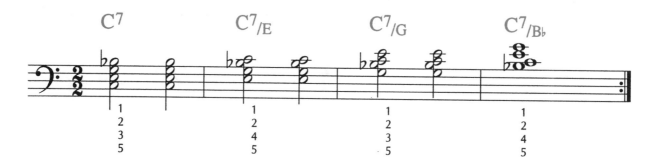

Cm7

A typical waltz pattern: the lowest note of the chord falls on the downbeat; the rest of the chord follows. "Sweet Molly," page 94, uses a simple variation of this broken-chord accompaniment. Depress the "loud" pedal on each downbeat to make a sustained sound.

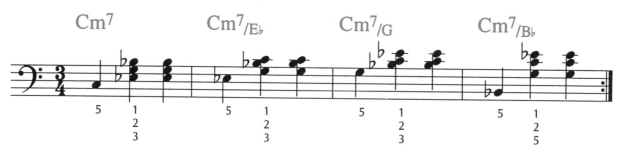

F7

This bouncy *note-chord/note-chord* pattern is a favorite all over the world, especially in lively folk dances and ragtime piano. To play it fast, practice it *slowly!*

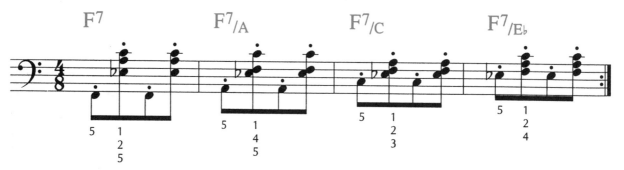

Fm⁷

The arpeggiated chord as a bass-line accompaniment is as common in jazz as it is in hundreds of classical pieces. "Etude in Blue," page 95, uses it in 8th notes.

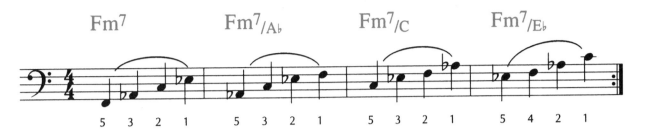

G⁷

A touch of Mozart: the so-called "Alberti bass" uses broken chords in gentle circular patterns, providing left-hand motion under quiet right-hand melodies. A lightly held pedal improves the keyboard sound.

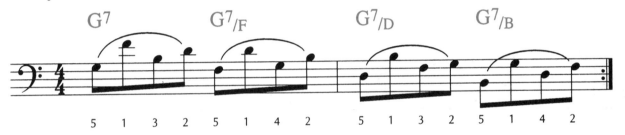

Gm⁷

Arpeggiated chords *divided between two hands* make a full sound, especially if you hold down the little finger at the start of each measure. "Ave Maria," page 100, is a perfect example of this fairly easy, good-sounding, hand-to-hand figuration.

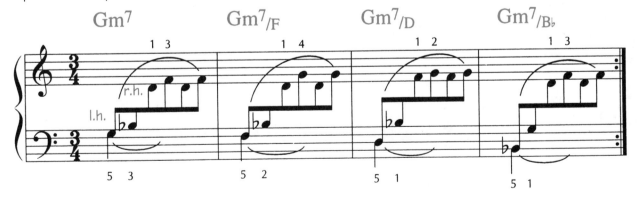

Quiet Meditation (III)
on "Black is the Color"

This lovely tune returns again, adding the rich, new coloration
of 7th chords in root position and various inversions.

Slow

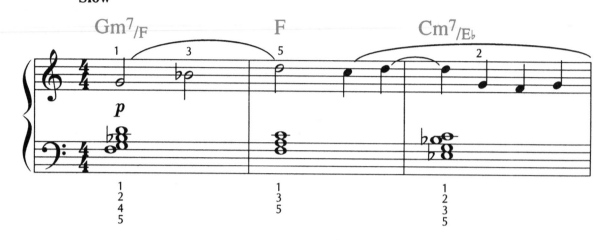

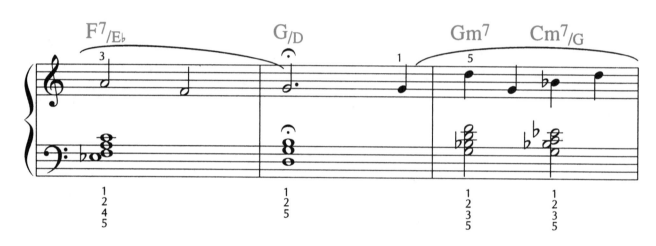

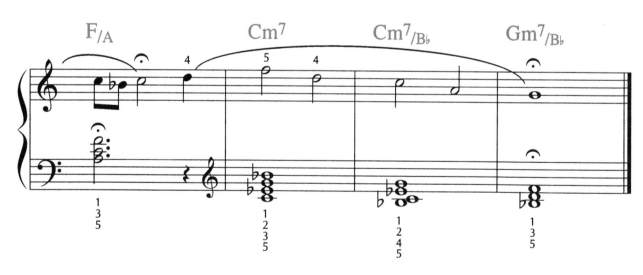

Quiet Meditation (IV)
on "Black is the Color"

A final visit with this Appalachian beauty, presenting the melody in the left hand
and the chordal background in the right — like "Quiet Meditation II," page 75.
This time, each empty red box is ready to be filled in with a missing chord symbol.
After you analyze each right-hand chord (ignore the left-hand notes),
write in your answer. (The first box is a free giveaway.)

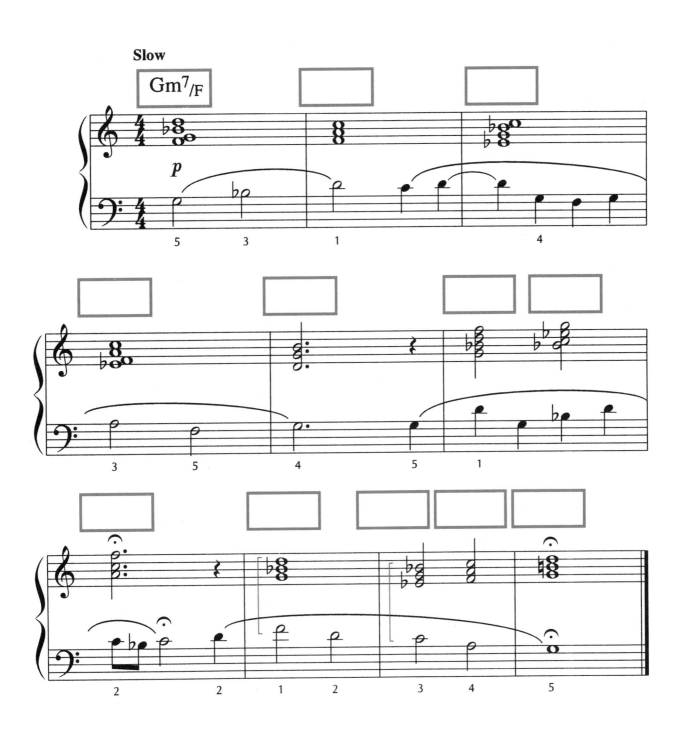

Sweet Molly
(Revisited)

The C⁷ and G⁷ chords are new additions to this favorite Irish tune you
first played on page 39. Listen to how they add color and a bit of
harmonic tension to the accompaniment.
This time, the left hand plays nothing but "broken" chords.

Etude in Blue

(Encore)

This is the same piece you played on page 47,
but now ALL of the chord symbols are properly filled in!
(The first version left out labels for the 7th chords.)

Slow and lazy

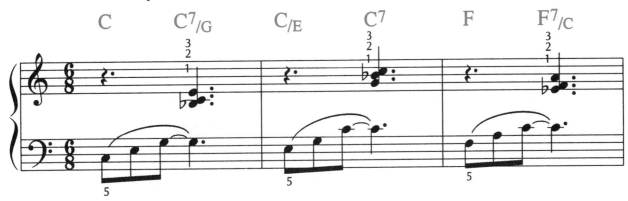

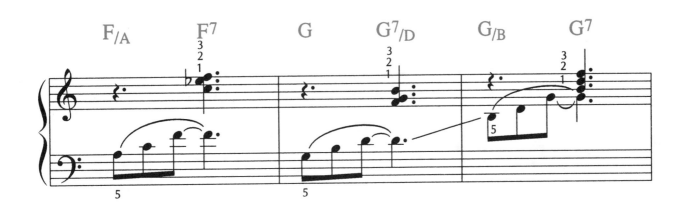

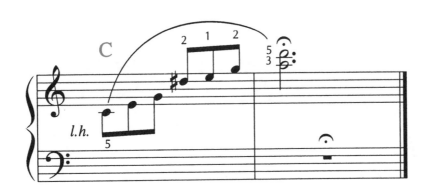

Grey Day, Strange Town

(Encore)

This intensified version of "Grey Day" builds up the music's
bluesy harmonies, changing triads to 7th chords in almost every bar.
The melody remains the same as in the original version on pages 78-79.

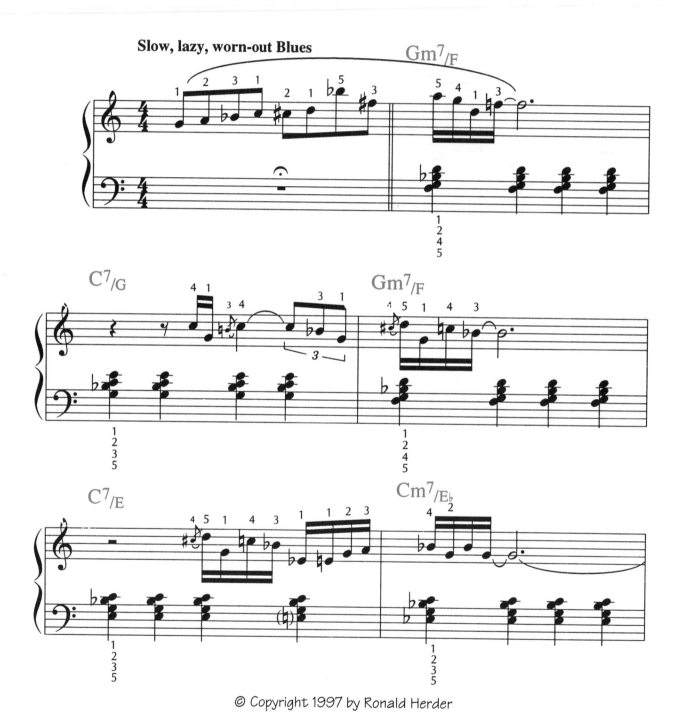

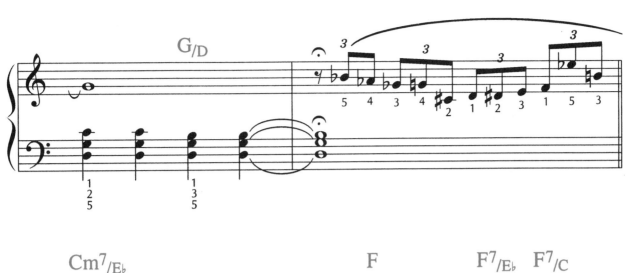

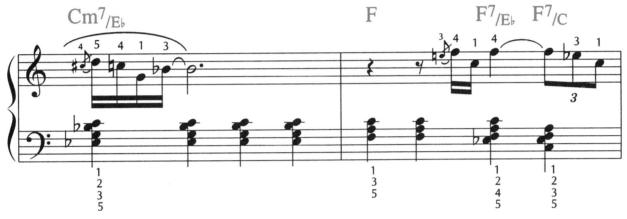

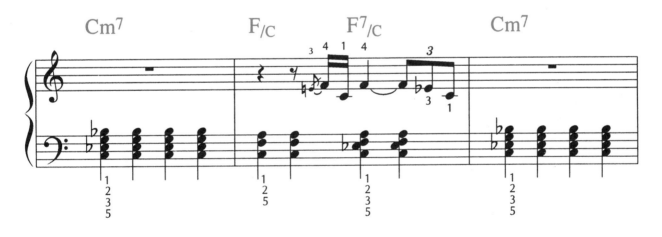

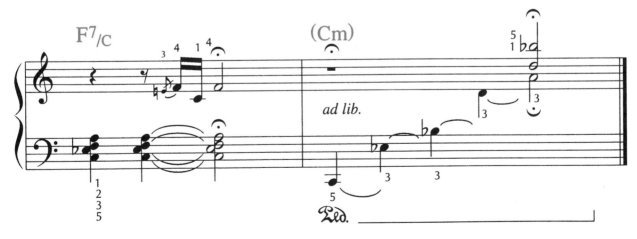

The St. Louis Blues

(Verse)

W.C. Handy

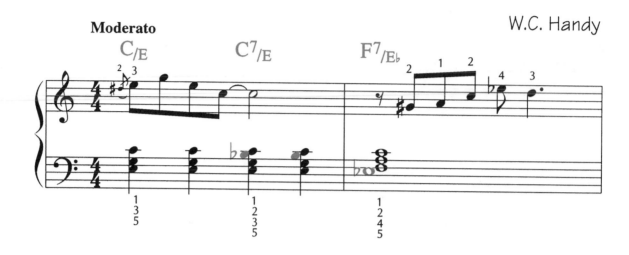

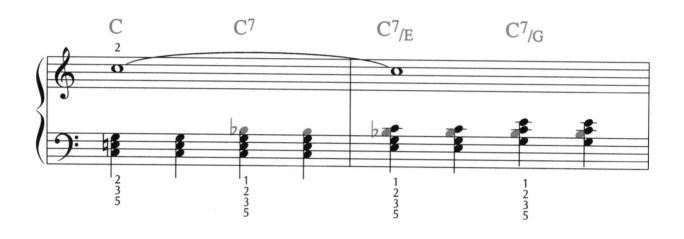

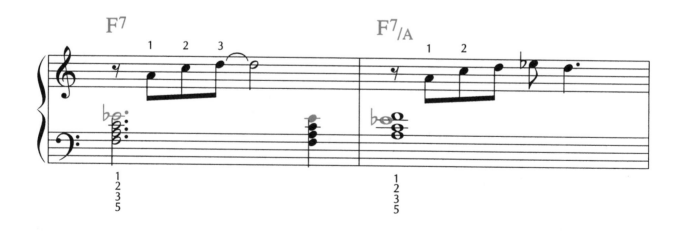

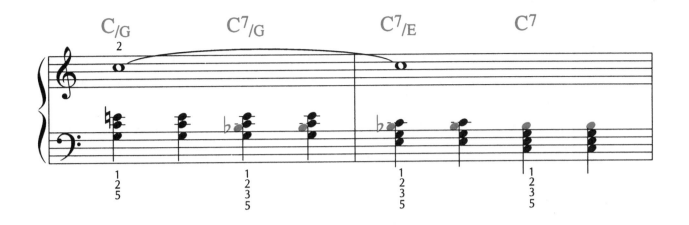

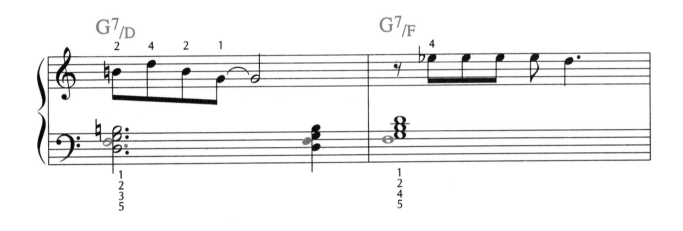

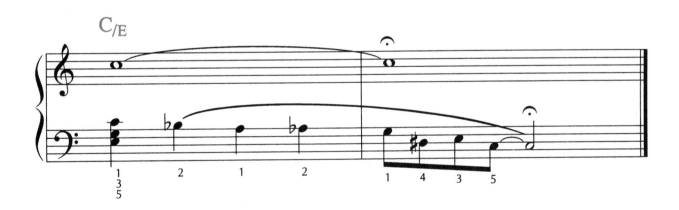

"Ave Maria" is an invitation to look backward and forward at the same time. "Backward," to everything you've taught yourself through the materials and ideas in this slim book. We hope you've reached this point with a satisfying feeling that you've achieved something good.

"Forward," to an advance look (a sneak preview!) into the colorful world of harmonies that can stretch your ears and your musicianship to distances beyond your imagination.

Most of the arpeggios in this final piece are built on familiar triads and seventh chords. Some are not. Some will look strange, with unfamiliar shapes and odd labels. But they are all part of an enormous world of musical harmony that invites you to go beyond this book, to explore and learn and experiment to your heart's content.

Ave Maria
(Meditation on a Prelude by Bach)

The trick here is to separate that sweet melody from the gentle arpeggios
that flow underneath it, forming its subdued accompaniment.
Those arpeggios are almost divided between the hands —
notes for the right hand are in the treble clef;
notes for the left hand are in the bass clef.

Accompaniment based on the Prelude in C from
Johann Sebastian Bach's *The Well-Tempered Clavier*, Book I.

Melody by Charles Gounod

Depress the pedal once for each bar.

"Foreign" note

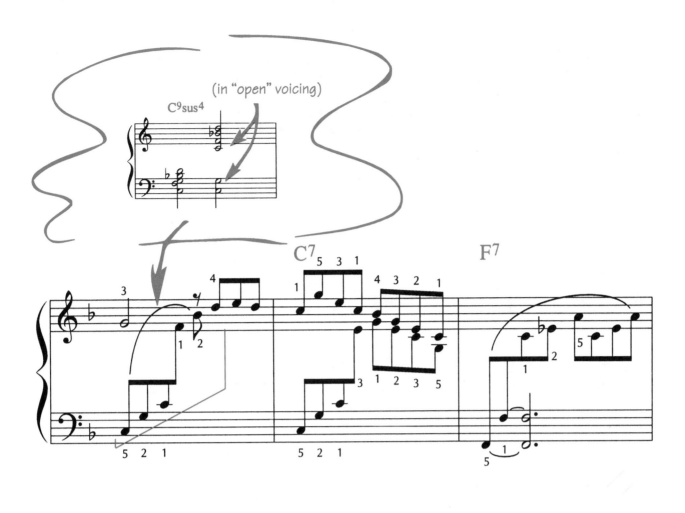

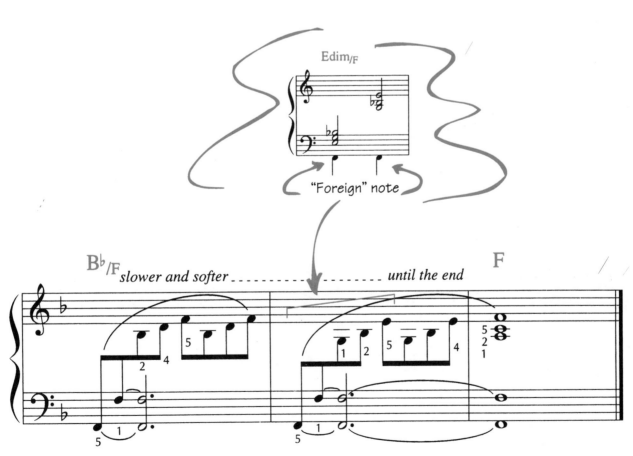

A GRAND CHART OF SIX TRIADS AND SIX 7TH CHORDS

A visual summary for quick and easy reference

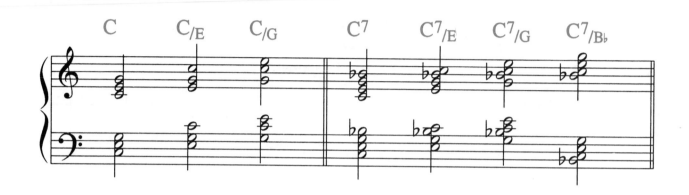

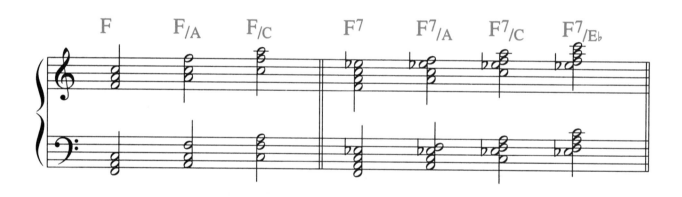

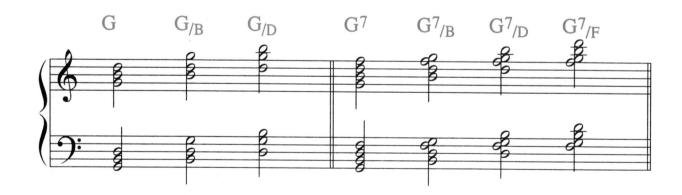

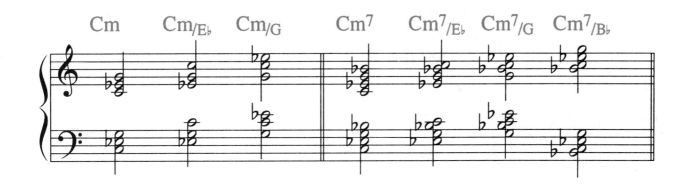

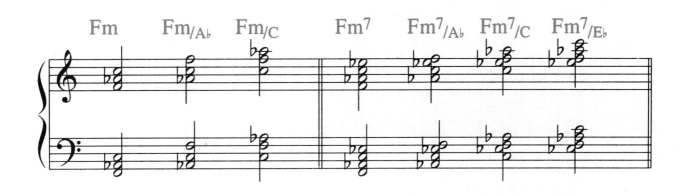

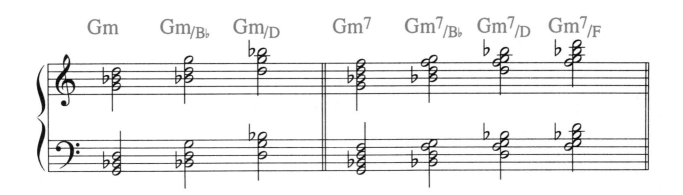

SONG LIST

A complete alphabetical list of the pieces in this volume